Amalgam Of Emotions

The heartfelt layers words can unveil...

Dr JK Sodhi

BookLeaf Publishing

India | USA | UK

Dedication

To my beloved parents *Mr. Bhupinder Singh Sodhi* and *Mrs. Cheena Sodhi* for giving me the gift of life and for teaching me kindness, resilience and strength. Your unwavering love, support and sacrifices shaped me into who i am and instilled in me the courage to follow my heart. I love you both beyond anything in the world and owe everything to you.

To my incredible spouse *Dr Manmeet Singh* for being my anchor and the light of my life *Seher.* Thank you for awakening within me a life and feelings i never knew had existed.

To my in laws *Dr. TP Singh, Mrs. Maninder kaur* and beyond just a sibling *Dr. KMS* for welcoming me with open arms and showing me warmth of their love.

Preface

Poetry is the language of soul and the silence between the words. It is an art which fills the void between what is said and what is felt. This collection is a reflection of journey through the landscapes of heart. From indescribable motherhood to strength of women, from pure joy to disappointments, from hope to belief, from nature to the virtual world, from beauty of subtle moments to the loud world...each poem within these pages attempts to capture the raw and delicate feelings. *Amalgam of emotions* embraces the full spectrum of feelings- both luminous and clouded...as that is what life is made of and in this beautiful amalgamation we live our lives whilst finding our inner self.

I hope these words resonate with your stories and remind you that the multifaceted emotions carried by our hearts are legitimate and add zest to our personal voyages. And this complex chaos is what makes our hearts whole .

Acknowledgements

I owe it to my *mother* who instilled in me the love for literature and my *father* who gave me wings to fly. I am indeed blessed to be their daughter!! Nothing would have ever been possible without them. I do appreciate my *better half* for the wind beneath my wings, for standing by my side and motivating me to be a better version of myself. I also thank my *limbic system* for letting me live and feel all the sentiments words can hold. And how can i forget the new addition in my life who painted my sky *pink* and made me feel it all more deeply. Forever grateful for my extended *inlaws* family for letting me pursue all i wanted through their encouragement and immense support. Last but not the least, filled with gratitude for whatever *lord almighty* has blessed me with.

The loud world

Soft soul in the world too loud,
She often whispered her secrets to the clouds,
Every now and then they poured down,
She gathered it all with the strength paramount,
She doubted herself for feeling too much,
And felt the world was superficial and pretender enough!
But isn't it a blessing in disguise?
To feel through the heart and read through the eyes,
Hence...
her heart carried it all and paid the price...

A letter to my daughter

I celebrated you before you arrived,
While the world whispered *'A son alone is pride'*
The world's outdated notions...all felt wrong,
Because with you my love is where my heart belonged,
You are my joy...my heart sings your name,
You are my world...my eternal flame,
I celebrated you...my heart's pride,
My precious little treasure with the brightest eyes,
Let no one perceive that you cannot stand,
My warrior princess you are made of fiercer sand,
Let the world doubt and let them ignore,
Rise above it all and like a lioness you roar!
Don't let this world decide your worth,
For you are a force and miracle of the earth!
At every step show them your might,
Shine in the dark and be the world's true light!
As your biggest cheerleader...I'll lift you high,
And let you fly with the wings that never die.

Solitude's embrace

In the tranquil hush i find my peace,
Wherein all desires of the made-up world cease,
No rush...no chaos...no words to say,
In that safe space i find my way,
No weights to carry and no one to please,
Just peace around and moments of ease,
No labels to place and no judgements to pass,
No expectations to fill and no race to surpass,
And in its folds i find my light,
The *solitude's embrace* wraps me tight.

Hopes set free

I occasionally sit with my younger self and feel,
The stars seem quieter now i believe,
The shadows fall differently and the clouds feel heavy,
I keep searching for colours i painted a bit too pretty,
The picture seems too gray now and my *hopes set free*,
My hands unlearning the weight of what was and
opening slowly to the light of what will be!!

An ode to women

Defined by a man and dictated by societal norms,
That's how a *woman's* life slowly transforms,
The day she is born there are seldom smiles,
For every validation ahead she has to walk a thousand
miles,
Freedom enjoys the man...
While pain is what she hides!!
Privileged is the man...
While she struggles for her side,
Pillar of creation and undefined love she is...
Whilst a man is the one who walks with pride,
How does one explain the inconceivable strength that
makes her...
To make her story discernible she takes long strides,
And the world dares to tell her all the things she cannot
be,
With the courage in her heart, determination in her
bones...she overrides every obstacle with pride!!

Heart's anguish

Seeing her cry... she cried more...
It stirred her heart and crushed her soul,
Soft sobs and welled up little eyes,
Red flushed face and those teeny tiny sighs!!
How could a mother behold all that goes inside?
Sighting the bawling of her little one...gaping her heart
wide,
Coz she loved the *little girl* more than her life!!

Pity

I pity those who fail to see,
A child's birth is a greatest plea,
Yet the day *'she'* arrives the world does sigh,
The *literate and civilized* one's question- "*Oh my god why?*"
In their eyes a son would be more right,
And they place *her* worth out of sight,
They create the rules for society to abide,
And pass their judgements with irrational pride,
I pity those who fail to know,
And realise in *her* new life will grow,
I pity them they fail to think,
The birth of a child is a blessing to sing,
For the miracle they are and the love they bring!

A little more

Let me love you *a little more*,
Until you are not little anymore!
Let me carry you a little longer,
Till you become bigger and stronger,
Let me cuddle you a bit more,
Let me look at you a little longer and adore,
Let me drench in the beauty of everything you are,
Let me cherish a bit more my miraculous rockstar,
Let me fall in love with your smile a little more,
Let me snuggle your little hands and toes,
Let me halt the time and make it last,
I want it to slow down but its going too fast!!
Never did i knew i could love so much,
Until the day you came and transformed my life with
your magical touch!

Nature

The chirping of birds...the first ray of morning light,
The cool breeze on a sunny day...the sun beaming bright,
The blooming flowers and the ravishing butterfly,
The leaves shimmering in the wind and the boundless
sky!
The ecstatic wildlife and the colours of rainbow,
The infinite sea and the mountains covered with snow!
The luscious fruits...a pure delight,
Beauty everywhere...angelic and refined,
Hence *nature* is a wonderous place with a surreal
splendor around,
A music for those who want to listen and hold the heart
spellbound!

Motherhood

No one shares when a baby is born,
How a woman's life forever transforms,
It feels as though she had two lives,
The second one begins when the baby arrives,
A part of her slyly fades away,
Her world spins around the 'lil one' each day,
Her own desires seem trivial dreams,
Though once upon a time they made her heart beam,
From phantom cries to anxiety and guilt,
That's how her second life is built,
Lost in the waves of relentless care,
She feels the challenge is for her alone to bear,
Through sleepless nights and endless days,
She finds her joys and finds her ways,
But in her child's eyes she sees the light,
And all the struggles feel so right,
She grows, evolves and gains her might,
And embraces the change in a softer light.

Belief

I *believed* you will see the pain through my eyes,
The stories they tell and the emotions they hide!
To watch over me tenderly when heavy felt the soul,
To embrace me in your arms when i needed the most,
To stand by me and listen to the tales i wanted to share,
To call and tell how you missed me and show me that
you cared,
To tell me how you felt like and how your day went,
To call me or write me about the moments you spent,
To tell me i look beautiful...even if its a lie,
To celebrate me for who i am and air my wings to fly,
To make me feel that i am loved, appreciated and whole,
To nurture my heart and fill my soul,
To make me *believe* in love more and more.

The greater love

Just when she thought she knew how love felt like,
Unsound it was proven by a gummy little smile,
Nurtured by the blood in her veins and water in her
womb,
A heart came to life inside and a miracle did bloom,
She ripped her body apart to bring it into the world,
Her insides were filled with light and the lines of reality
grew blurred,
It reshaped her soul in the way unbelievable,
The sleepless nights, the silent sacrifices and the
boundless love...it all felt inconceivable!
Little did she knew her heart wont be her own,
That no love would feel greater than her child...the most
beautiful bond!!

Disappointment

Believer i was...you will be a forever home to my heart,
Time debunked my beliefs and we drifted apart,
In seeking your love i lost my way,
The hard revelation did leave me stray,
Expectations they say foster regret,
And in that gamble my heart did bet,
Yet in that adrift i did hear,
The echoes of life loud and clear,
That 'No...a person cannot be your home',
Heart's quiet place is in our soul's deep dome.

My girl

Lying pleasantly drowsy the cry reached my ears,
Flooding me with emotions it allayed all my fears,
"It's a girl" i heard the doctor's voice,
It brightened up my soul... numbing all the extra noise,
My prayers were answered and my heart was full,
My skies were coloured and my life became all beautiful,
Within a little while my world did transmute,
Little hands and tiny little feet....absolutely cute!!
My girl arrived and was laying besides me,
I thank god incessantly for this boundless glee!!

Trying to hold on but barely...

All by myself i do reflect at night,
Maybe my thoughts and solitude are my only light,
My soul yearns for love and tender compassion,
No materialistic things...maybe a bit old fashioned!
Time, love and care is all i need to thrive,
But my soul seems to wither away while trying to stay alive,
Beneath the sky or in the quite room your presence fades,
My soul keeps on searching for it till the end of the day,
Silence misunderstood...words unsaid...my soul deprived,
In your company alone it hides,
Alone it strives alone it feels,
This solitude i am *trying to hold on* till i learn to heal.

Music of my soul

Nothing so delightful i ever found,
The song of her laughter lifts me off the ground,
That bright and pure bare-toothed smile,
Makes every moment worthwhile,
The pinching up of her nose and the twinkle in her eyes,
That heartiest chuckle makes my heart go wild!
Her joyful giggle...music of my soul,
Makes me fall in love once more,
deeper and deeper more than before...

Allied

Whatever you plan or plan for the coming precious time,
Nothing will heal the wounds i carried in this moment of
prime,
All adds onto it...either past or present,
Full of pain and all numb i feel...my soul sickened!
You know me no longer, nor do i...
Strangers we are...just together and *allied*,
I wanted the unreasonable...time...love and care,
Varied priorities....ignorant of me to be unaware

Subtle moments

Subtle moments in life play their part,
Taking up the most space in our hearts,
Seldom kind words that strangers impart,
Brightens up the heart's darkest parts,
An unexpected compliment at random times,
Imprints on the heart for longtime,
A shared smile in a jam packed place,
Makes it easier to face the world with grace,
Unjudged notions by our nears and dears,
Love and acceptance by our peers,
Silent moments with no one besides,
Whilst the world in chaotic and loud outside,
A handwritten note like old days,
Just thoughts poured out...no fleeting pace,
Joy reflected upon parents face,
Subtle thing...but a moment's grace,
For such fleeting moments that seem so light,
Lies surge of happiness and unseen delight!

My heart

Feels like *my heart* is walking outside,
Wherein skies stretch far and emotions collide,
With *her* every laughter and every tear,
Vulnerable feels the heart...all exposed and bare,
With my each breath...a whisper of prayer,
Guarded by love and relentless care,
Yet i've never smiled so much...you see,
Since the day she became a part of me,
And i've never smiled so much...that's true,
In her light...i found my hue!

The virtual world

Astounded indeed, how people neglect too soon,
These moments...this time is nothing less than a boon,
Eyes glued to *screens*...their fingers scroll up and down,
Overlooking the incalculable beauty awaiting around,
The majestic nature.... the limitless sky,
The benevolent family awaiting by,
Life is short and time is swift,
Beholden the beauty around and all the bliss!

Eyes

Those beautiful glimmery wide red *eyes*,
Pointed at something and tried to vocalise,
The helplessness and pain in the heart,
The melancholic mind and soul torn apart.
Who could have portrayed it all?
Eyes....Indeed a work of art!

www.ingramcontent.com/pod-product-compliance
Lightning Source LLC
LaVergne TN
LVHW021356200726
843509LV00014B/2890